CONNECTIONS

FLORENCE NIGHTINGALE

Stewart Ross

Evans Brothers Limited

First published in this edition in 2010

Published by Evans Brothers Limited
2A Portman Mansions
Chiltern Street
London W1U 6NR

Produced for Evans Brothers Limited by
White-Thomson Publishing Ltd.,
+44 (0) 843 2087 460
www.wtpub.co.uk

Printed & bound in China by New Era Printing
Company Limited

Editor: Dereen Taylor
Consultants: Nina Siddall, Head of Primary School
Improvement, East Sussex; Norah Granger, former
primary head teacher and senior lecturer in Education,
University of Brighton; Kate Ruttle, freelance literacy
consultant and Literacy Co-ordinator, Special Needs
Co-ordinator, and Deputy Headteacher at a primary
school in Suffolk.
Designer: Leishman Design
Cover design: Balley Design Limited

The right of Stewart Ross to be identified as the author of
this work has been asserted by him inaccordance with the
Copyright, Designs and Patents Act 1988.

British Library Cataloguing in Publication Data

Ross, Stewart.
    Florence Nightingale. -- (Start-up connections)
    1. Nightingale, Florence, 1820-1910--Juvenile literature.
    2. Nurses--England--Biography--Juvenile literature.
    3. Crimean War, 1853-1856--Medical care--Great
        Britain--   Juvenile literature.
    I. Title II. Series
    610.7'3'092-dc22

ISBN: 978 0 237 54170 5

Acknowledgements: The publishers would like to thank
the Florence Nightingale Museum, London, for their
assistance with this book.

Picture Acknowledgements: Bridgeman Art Library
9 (right); Bridgeman Art Library/British Museum 8;
Bridgeman Art Library/Private Collection cover (centre),
10 (top), 12 (bottom), 15; Corbis 17, 19 (right); Florence
Nightingale Museum 11, 18; Fotomas Index 19 (left);
Mary Evans Picture Library (cover, top right) 4, 5, 9 (top),
10 (bottom), 12 (top), 13, 14; P&O Art Collection 7;
Topham Picturepoint 16.

Contents

Florence Nightingale, a famous nurse

► **This is Florence Nightingale.
She was born long ago, in the year 1820.**

How are her clothes different from modern clothes?

long ago   year   modern

▲ **Florence** was a famous nurse.
She worked in hospitals like this one.

famous   nurse   hospitals

Florence goes to help

In 1854, **Great Britain** went to **war with Russia**. The war was far away, in the **Crimea**.

Florence went to nurse the **injured soldiers**.

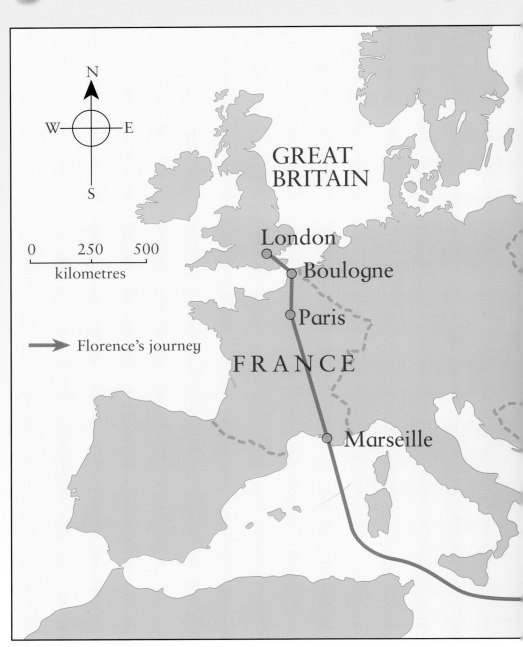

N
W — E
S

0   250   500
kilometres

→ Florence's journey

GREAT BRITAIN

London
Boulogne
Paris

FRANCE

Marseille

RUSSIA

Crimean
Battlefields

Balaklava

BLACK SEA

Scutari

TURKEY

MEDITERRANEAN SEA

◀ **This map shows her journey. She travelled by land and sea.**

▼ **Florence sailed in this ship.**

injured   soldiers   map   sailed   **7**
......

Why did Florence go to the war?

▼ This is a painting of a battle in the Crimean War. What weapons are the soldiers using?

painting   battle

▲ This soldier is helping his friend who has been hurt.

Nurses were needed at the war.

▶ This man, Sidney Herbert, asked Florence to go and help. She said "yes" straight away.

weapons   hurt

Florence and the horrible hospital

► This is the hospital where Florence worked. It was in a place called Scutari.

Scutari was a long way from the Crimea.

◄ Injured soldiers went to Scutari by boat.

Scutari   boat

▼ This is the inside of a hospital during the war.

Scutari hospital looked like this, too.
It was crowded, dirty and smelly.
How many injured soldiers can you see?

crowded   dirty   smelly

Florence goes to work

► Florence needed medicines from Britain. They were sent by ship.

◄ Queen Victoria helped Florence. She sent kind words and presents for the soldiers.

medicines

▼ **Here is Florence talking to a soldier in Scutari Hospital.**

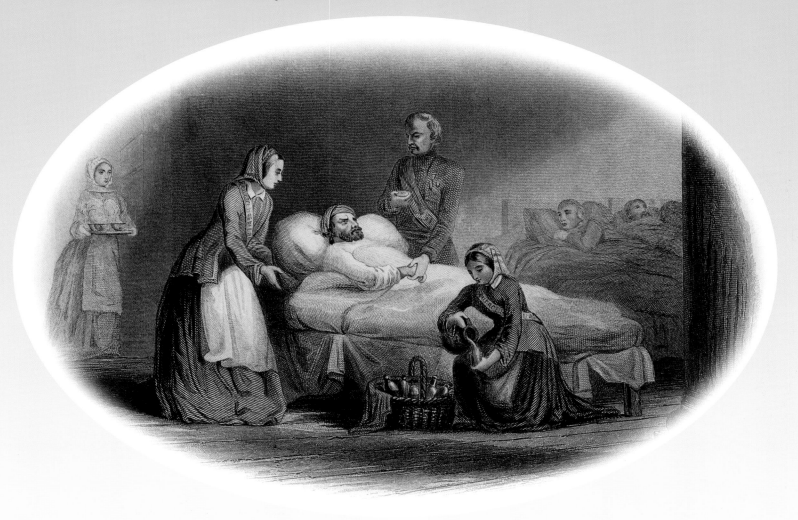

She worked to make it **cleaner** and **healthier**.
How is the hospital in this picture different
from the picture of the hospital on page 11?

cleaner   **healthier**

How did Florence help?

▲ This is the inside of Scutari hospital after Florence had cleaned it up.

There are clean sheets on the beds and a stove to keep the patients warm.

patients

Florence trained other nurses at Scutari.
▼ **This nurse is working near a battle.**

How can you tell that this photograph
was taken long ago?

trained   photograph   15

Nursing changes

After she returned from the war, Florence started a school for nurses.

Here is Florence with some of the nurses from her school. The nurses are wearing their uniforms.

16

This is a nurse at work today.
She is wearing a plastic apron.

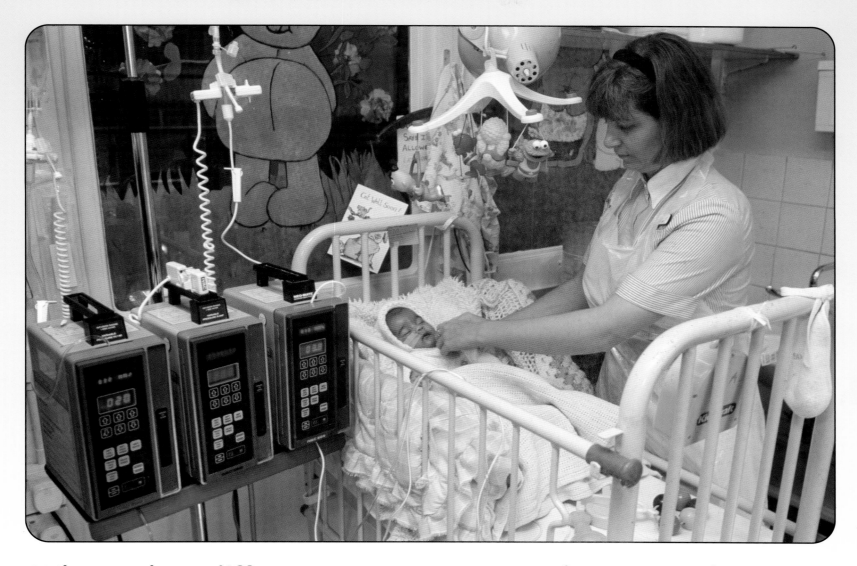

What other differences can you see between this
picture and the pictures of the hospitals from the past?

today   plastic   differences   past   17

How do we know about Florence Nightingale?

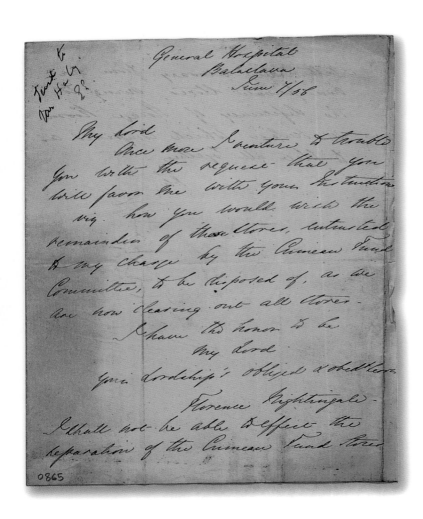

Florence Nightingale **died** almost 100 years ago.

We can find out about Florence by reading the **letters** she wrote.

◄ This is a letter Florence wrote to Sidney Herbert from Balaklava.
You can find Balaklava on the map on pages 6 and 7.

died   **letters**

▲ **Newspapers and magazines from long ago tell us about Florence.**

▼ **We can learn about Florence from old paintings and photographs, too.**

newspapers   magazines   19

The story of

Use these pictures and words to tell the story of Florence Nightingale.

nurse sailed Crimea soldier war

Florence Nightingale

Where did she go?

What did she do there?

Why do we remember her today?

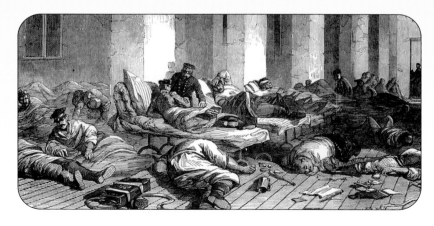

hospital   cleaner   Scutari   school

Further information for Parents and Teachers

FLORENCE NIGHTINGALE ACTIVITY PAGE

Use the activities on these pages to help you to make the most of *Florence Nightingale*.

Activities suggested on this page support progression in learning by consolidating and developing ideas from the book and helping the children to link the new concepts with their own experiences. Making these links is crucial in helping young children to engage with learning and to become lifelong learners.

Ideas on the next page develop essential skills for learning by suggesting ways of making links across the curriculum and in particular to literacy, personal development and ICT.

WORD PANEL

Check that the children know the meaning of each of these words from the book.

after	dirty	modern	Scutari
battle	famous	nurse	today
clean	healthy	painting	trained
Crimea	hospital	patient	uniform
crowded	injured	photograph	
different	long ago	same	

DIFFERENT TIMES

Help the children to understand that different times in history had different opinions about what different people should do.

- Do children know what their own parents do as their jobs, if they are employed? Can they name other jobs that grown-ups do?
- Seek ideas about what the children want to be when they grow up
- What do they need to do to be able to do the jobs they want to do?
- How would they feel if they weren't allowed to do the job because they were too tall or too short? Or the wrong gender? Or too rich or too poor?
- Establish that in different times and different places, people sometimes couldn't do the jobs they wanted to do no matter how hard they worked. How do children feel about that?
- Florence Nightingale's family didn't want her to be a nurse because she was too rich and nurses had to be from poor families.

Talk about what might have been different if Florence Nightingale hadn't been a nurse.

MARY SEACOLE

Mary Seacole was a Jamaican nurse who also helped soldiers in the Crimean War.

- Ask the children to find out about her using the internet.
- What did she do that helped the soldiers?
- Compare the contributions of Florence Nightingale and Mary Seacole.

DOCTORS AND NURSES

Establish the roles that doctors and nurses have today.

- Try to organise visits from a range of visitors who can talk about different aspects of doctors and nurses today. Before the visits, prepare the children to ask questions.
- Find photographs and video clips of modern hospitals, including military hospitals.
- Let the children use the new information and compare it to information in the book about hospitals, doctors and nurses.
- What is the same and what is different?

CRIMEAN WAR

What kind of questions can the children think of to find out more about the Crimean War?

- Let them work in groups to agree questions. If necessary, provide them with question starters eg Why did…. What did …. Where was …
- Once each group has established one or two questions, encourage members of the group to ask other children to see if anyone already knows an answer.
- If possible, arrange a visit to the nearest public library. Ask for a children's librarian to be available to show the children the resources in the library and to help them to find appropriate books to answer their questions, or to support them when they go online to find answers.
- Remind the children that they can find a lot of information from looking at pictures as well as by reading the text.

USING FLORENCE NIGHTINGALE FOR CROSS CURRICULAR WORK

The revised national curriculum focuses on children developing key competencies as

- successful learners
- confident individuals and
- responsible citizens.

Cross curricular work is particularly beneficial in developing the thinking and learning skills that contribute to building these competencies because it encourages children to make links, to

transfer learning skills and to apply knowledge from one context to another. As importantly, cross curricular work can help children to understand how school work links to their daily lives. For many children, this is a key motivation in becoming a learner.

The web below indicates some areas for cross curricular study. Others may well come from your own class's engagement with the ideas in the book.

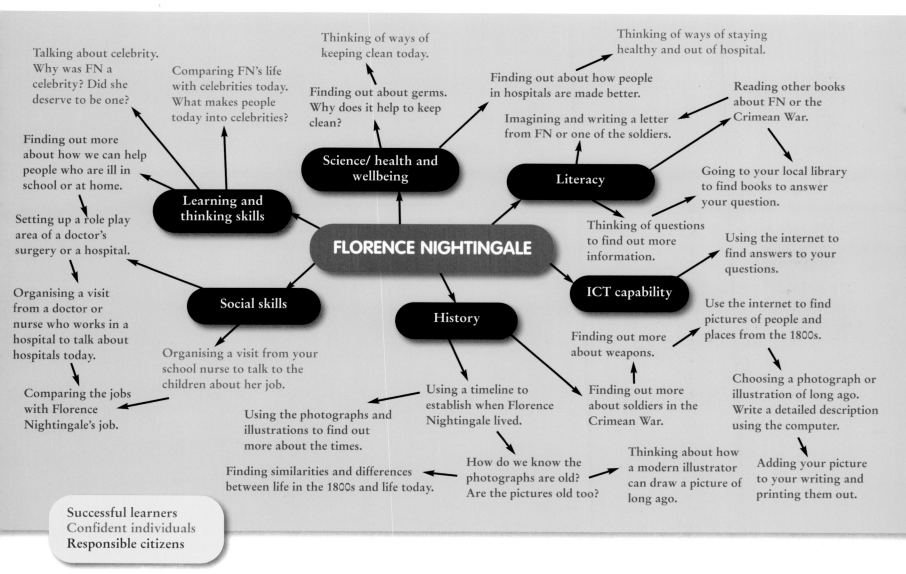

Talking about celebrity. Why was FN a celebrity? Did she deserve to be one?

Comparing FN's life with celebrities today. What makes people today into celebrities?

Thinking of ways of keeping clean today.

Finding out about germs. Why does it help to keep clean?

Thinking of ways of staying healthy and out of hospital.

Finding out about how people in hospitals are made better.

Reading other books about FN or the Crimean War.

Finding out more about how we can help people who are ill in school or at home.

Setting up a role play area of a doctor's surgery or a hospital.

Learning and thinking skills

Science/ health and wellbeing

Imagining and writing a letter from FN or one of the soldiers.

Literacy

Going to your local library to find books to answer your question.

FLORENCE NIGHTINGALE

Thinking of questions to find out more information.

Using the internet to find answers to your questions.

Organising a visit from a doctor or nurse who works in a hospital to talk about hospitals today.

Social skills

History

ICT capability

Use the internet to find pictures of people and places from the 1800s.

Finding out more about weapons.

Comparing the jobs with Florence Nightingale's job.

Organising a visit from your school nurse to talk to the children about her job.

Using a timeline to establish when Florence Nightingale lived.

Finding out more about soldiers in the Crimean War.

Choosing a photograph or illustration of long ago. Write a detailed description using the computer.

Using the photographs and illustrations to find out more about the times.

How do we know the photographs are old? Are the pictures old too?

Thinking about how a modern illustrator can draw a picture of long ago.

Adding your picture to your writing and printing them out.

Finding similarities and differences between life in the 1800s and life today.

Successful learners
Confident individuals
Responsible citizens

23

Index